Original title:
Snowy Solace

Copyright © 2024 Swan Charm
All rights reserved.

Author: Paula Raudsepp
ISBN HARDBACK: 978-9916-79-300-8
ISBN PAPERBACK: 978-9916-79-301-5
ISBN EBOOK: 978-9916-79-302-2

Ethereal Blankets

Whispers in the twilight glow,
Softly falling, magic slow.
Each flake a story, pure and bright,
Cocooning earth in tender light.

Glistening under silver rays,
Nature dances, lost in praise.
A world transformed, serene and wide,
In this hush, our hearts confide.

The Solace of Winter Nights

Starry blankets, soft and deep,
Crickets hush, the world's asleep.
Fires crackle, warmth so near,
In this moment, dreams appear.

Frosted panes tell tales untold,
Whispered secrets, hearts unfold.
Underneath the vast expanse,
We find peace in winter's dance.

A Frosted Dreamscape

Snowflakes twirl in graceful flight,
Transforming earth to pure delight.
Footprints trace a path so clear,
In this wonderland, we steer.

Trees adorned in icy lace,
Every branch a quiet grace.
A frozen world, serene and calm,
In nature's arms, we find our balm.

Echoes Beneath the Snow

Silent echoes, whispers low,
Memories dance beneath the snow.
Each step taken, soft and slight,
Guided by the pale moonlight.

Frozen tales from times long past,
In this stillness, shadows cast.
The world holds its breath, in wait,
For spring to whisper, to create.

Frosting the Memory

Whispers of laughter, sweet and clear,
Echoes of days we held so dear.
Softly they glisten, like fresh snowflakes,
Carving our moments, as stillness wakes.

Each glance a treasure, wrapped in light,
Captured in time, like stars at night.
Frosting the edges, memories swell,
Layers of joy, in stories we tell.

The Softness of the Dusk

As the sun dips low, the sky ignites,
Painting the world in mellow lights.
Veils of lavender drift through the trees,
In the embrace of a gentle breeze.

Whispers of night creep over the land,
Softness surrounding, a gentle hand.
The horizon blushes, a fleeting grace,
In the calm of dusk, we find our place.

Shadows Beneath the Ice

Beneath the surface, secrets reside,
Shadows that dance with nowhere to hide.
Frozen echoes of laughter and fears,
Trapped in a world that forgets its tears.

Glimmers of hope pierce the cold blue,
Whispers of warmth in the silent view.
Under the ice, the stories remain,
Waiting to surface, like drops of rain.

Winter's Tranquil Palette

A canvas of white, brushed with grey,
Winter unfolds in a gentle sway.
Soft footprints wander, tracing the ground,
In the stillness, a peace profound.

With each falling flake, a hush descends,
Nature's embrace, where time suspends.
Colors of frost mingle with light,
A tranquil palette, serene and bright.

From Darkness to Soft Illumination

In shadows deep, where whispers sigh,
A flicker glows, a hopeful cry.
From cold despair, we rise anew,
Embraced by light, a warm debut.

The night retreats, the stars align,
In tender hues, our souls entwine.
Through tangled paths, we find our way,
To brighter dawns, to love's ballet.

The Chronicles of a Frozen Heart

Beneath the ice, where feelings sleep,
A tale unfolds, the heart's deep keep.
With every breath, the frost will fade,
And secrets bloom, in warmth arrayed.

A silent cry, a longing flush,
In winter's grip, there lies a hush.
Yet in this cold, a spark will rise,
Transforming pain into the skies.

Secrets Held in the Frost

Crystal whispers in the air,
Frozen secrets everywhere.
Each flake that falls, a tale to tell,
Of dreams in slumber, cast in spell.

The chill wraps snug, yet hope is near,
In glistening frost, we find no fear.
With every dawn, the truth will shine,
Unraveling mysteries, divine design.

Winter's Tapestry of Solitude

In stillness dwells a quilt of white,
Where silence reigns in pure delight.
Each flake a thread of timeless grace,
We weave our dreams in this still space.

Alone yet whole, the heart takes flight,
In winter's arms, we find our light.
In solitude, we learn to see,
The beauty wrapped in sacred glee.

Tender Moments in the Chill

Gentle breezes softly sigh,
Among the trees, the shadows lie.
Fingers brush and hearts awake,
In chilly air, sweet warmth we make.

Snowflakes dance, a breathless waltz,
Holding tightly, love absolves.
In this moment, time stands still,
With whispered dreams, our hearts to fill.

Through crisp nights, the fire glows,
Under stars, our laughter flows.
Embraced by winter's tender grace,
In silent nights, we find our place.

Each shared glance, a spark divine,
In the cold, our souls entwine.
With every shiver, a secret spark,
Illuminates our winter's dark.

Tender moments, fleeting, bright,
Nestled close in quilted night.
With every heartbeat, we believe,
In the chill, our love will weave.

The Stillness of Crystal Air

In the hush of silent nights,
Crystals glimmer, capturing lights.
A breath held tight in frosty gleam,
Reality fades into a dream.

Footprints whisper on the ground,
In the stillness, peace is found.
Nature's canvas, pure and bright,
Painted gently in soft white.

Branches laden with snowy lace,
Twinkling stars, a cosmic embrace.
Underneath the silver sky,
We hold moment, swaying by.

Breath of winter, crisp and clear,
Every heartbeat draws you near.
In the calm, the world is vast,
Within this still, our dreams are cast.

Gathered close 'neath moon's soft glance,
In crystal air, we take our chance.
With every whisper, love ignites,
The stillness breathes, the heart unites.

Heartbeats in the Frost

In the silence of the frost,
Every warmth feels like a cost.
Yet here we stand, souls alive,
Together, we learn to survive.

Crimson cheeks and laughter bright,
In chill air, we hold on tight.
With every heartbeat, bold and free,
A symphony of you and me.

Frosty mornings, whispers low,
Where love and winter intertwine slow.
Each moment touches like the snow,
A gentle kiss, a tender flow.

Glistening paths where footsteps tread,
For every doubt, our hearts are fed.
With every breath, the world expands,
In frozen realms, we make our plans.

In icy nights, stars alight,
Together, we step into the night.
Heartbeats in the frost, we trust,
In winter's touch, our love is just.

Whispers of Winter's Embrace

Whispers float on frosty air,
Soft confessions, secrets rare.
In every flake that falls so light,
Lies a promise of our night.

Wrapped in warmth, the world feels new,
In our haven, just us two.
Snowdrifts cradle dreams untold,
In winter's arms, love grows bold.

With every chill, a heart ignites,
Fires crackle on starry nights.
Through the stillness, we create,
A tapestry of love and fate.

Echoes dance in the silent wood,
Underneath skies, where few have stood.
Hand in hand, through the frost we roam,
In winter's whisper, we find home.

So let the world wear icy grace,
In every moment, we embrace.
For in these whispers, love's laid bare,
In winter's clutch, we find our prayer.

Journey Through the Quiet Drift

Whispers float on the breeze,
Footprints fade in the snow,
Each step tells its own tale,
As the quiet rivers flow.

Branches cradle the stars,
Wrapped in a soft embrace,
The moon guides the way,
With her gentle, silver grace.

Frost kisses the silent woods,
Time stands still in this dream,
Every shimmer a secret,
In the twilight's sunbeam.

Paths intertwine with shadows,
Nature's breath, a soft sigh,
Lost in the tranquil moments,
As the night meets the sky.

Through stillness, peace is found,
A journey we all must take,
In the heart of the quiet,
We awaken, we awake.

An Artisan of Snowflakes

In the silence of winter,
Beauty dances in the cold,
Each flake tells a story,
A masterpiece to behold.

Crafted by unseen hands,
With delicate, frosty lace,
They swirl and spin through the air,
In nature's fine embrace.

No two are ever the same,
Like thoughts in a winter chill,
Glistening under the sun,
Each unique, a gentle thrill.

They blanket the world in white,
Transforming all with their art,
A fleeting moment of grace,
Capturing the world's heart.

In their quiet descent,
Lies a promise, so serene,
An artisan's hidden touch,
In this framed, winter dream.

Choreography of Cold and Quiet

The air is crisp and clear,
While shadows pirouette,
In the dance of winter's chill,
Each move perfect, no regret.

Snowflakes twirl like dancers,
Spinning in the frosted light,
Nature's graceful ballet,
A wondrous, tranquil sight.

Branches sway in rhythm,
To the heartbeat of the breeze,
A silent symphony plays,
Comfort found in the freeze.

Footsteps create the tempo,
Echoing on the ground,
In this choreography,
Harmony can be found.

Pause and breathe in the still,
Let the moment ignite,
As winter's art unfolds,
In the purest, soft light.

Beneath the Blanket of Stillness

A world wrapped in silence,
Lies beneath the soft snow,
Cradled in winter's arms,
Where the cool breezes blow.

Time seems to hold its breath,
As stars flicker above,
The whisper of the night,
Softened by the moon's love.

Nature rests in repose,
In the quiet of the night,
Every shadow listens close,
To the heart of pure light.

Underneath this stillness,
Life waits, patient and true,
Dreams hidden in the frost,
Awaiting blooms anew.

Embrace the depth of silence,
Let the stillness unfold,
For beneath that quiet cover,
A new story is told.

A Reverie in the Winter's Pause

In silent woods where shadows creep,
Snowflakes weave a tale so deep.
Whispers of the trees in sighs,
Beneath the vast and open skies.

A blanket white on every stone,
The chill envelops all alone.
Footprints mark the path of dreams,
Caught in soft, reflective beams.

The world is hushed, time takes a breath,
In frozen beauty, life and death.
Memories swirl like flakes in flight,
These moments held in purest light.

The distant brook shows icy grace,
Cradling nature's soft embrace.
In winter's pause, the heart can rest,
In tranquil bliss, we feel our best.

And as the stars begin to gleam,
In silent night, we find our dream.
With every breath, a soft release,
In winter's grasp, we hold our peace.

The Epic of a Quiet Blizzard

White warriors dance on winter's call,
They gather close, they rise, they fall.
A swirling cloak of frosty might,
A tale of tempest wrapped in white.

The howl of wind, a ghostly choir,
With each gust, the senses tire.
Trees bow down, their branches bend,
Whispers lost, yet all shall mend.

Time draws thick as drifts arise,
A world transformed, the softest guise.
Vision fades to shades of gray,
As night embraces the waning day.

Yet in this storm, a warmth ignites,
The heart remembers cozy nights.
Inside the walls, laughter flows,
As outside, gentle chaos grows.

Together we watch the world unfold,
The epic dance as stories told.
Amidst the din, we find our fate,
In quiet moments that we await.

Muffled Echoes in the Snow

Steps are hushed on winter trails,
Echoes fade where silence prevails.
In the glow of twilight's grace,
Snowy whispers find their place.

Each flake a memory drifting down,
A soft blanket over sleepy town.
The world transformed in pale embrace,
As darkness steals the sun's warm face.

Chimneys breathe their gentle steam,
In homes where hearts and hopes can dream.
Outside, the air is crisp and clear,
Muffled voices draw us near.

Fires crackle, shadows play,
Time dances in a slow ballet.
The stillness holds us in its thrall,
Muffled echoes of a distant call.

In every drift and every sigh,
We find a moment that won't die.
In winter's touch, we come alive,
In echoes deep, our thoughts survive.

The Peaceful Eye of the Storm

In the center, calm and bright,
Winds howling, yet there's light.
Chaos spins all around,
A sheltered moment found.

Clouds collide, a fierce ballet,
Nature's dance in wild display.
Yet within this swirling tide,
A tranquil heart, a quiet guide.

The tempest rages, fierce and loud,
But here, the eye stands proud.
Breath deep, in this pause we stay,
Finding peace before the fray.

Fleeting Moments of White

Snowflakes drift on whispered breeze,
Dressing earth with gentle ease.
Each flake, a story spun,
Glittering under the waning sun.

A hush falls on the sleeping ground,
Nature frozen, beauty found.
Yet as they fall, they fade away,
Moments lost, just a day.

Chill of air, yet hearts feel warm,
These whispers of winter charm.
Capture well these lovely sights,
Fleeting moments of pure white.

Solitude in a Sea of Frost

Amidst the ice, I stand alone,
Silent echoes, a quiet tone.
Each breath hangs in the air,
In this solitude, I find my care.

Footprints lead where few have trod,
Upon the frozen, sacred sod.
Nature's artwork, cold and grand,
A world untouched by human hand.

The stillness wraps like a soft embrace,
In the frosty grip, I find my place.
Whispers of winter call to me,
In solitude, I am free.

Melodies of a Frozen World

Icicles hang like crystal chimes,
Singing softly through the pines.
The air hums with winter's tune,
Beneath the watchful, silver moon.

Frozen streams, a gentle song,
Nature's notes, both sweet and strong.
In this symphony of cold,
Stories of the earth unfold.

Each flake a note, each breath a rhyme,
In this frozen world, we find the time.
Listen close, let your heart unfurl,
To the melodies of a frozen world.

The Tranquil Frost

A blanket white across the ground,
Silence echoes, calm surrounds.
The world in a peaceful slumber,
Under stars, all dreams encumber.

The trees are draped in glistening sheen,
Whispers of nature, soft and keen.
Each breath is mist, a fleeting ghost,
In this stillness, we find our host.

Footsteps crunch on icy trails,
Through frosty woods, the heart exhales.
Moonlight dances on the snow,
A glowing path where wishes flow.

Beneath the sky, so deep and vast,
Every moment, a shadow cast.
In the chill, we find our grace,
Embracing winter's warm embrace.

Whispers from the Ice

Listen closely, hear the sound,
Secrets shared from icy ground.
The chill carries tales of old,
Of winter nights and hearts so bold.

Frosted whispers weave through trees,
Carried gently by the breeze.
In the hush, stories unfurl,
Silent dreams in a frozen swirl.

Glistening crystals, a world anew,
Painting scenes in glimmering hue.
Each flake a note, in harmony,
Creating winter's symphony.

Paths of ice stretch far and wide,
A serene canvas where thoughts hide.
In the quiet, we find release,
In the frost, we discover peace.

Dreaming in a Winter Realm

Snowflakes fall, a gentle sigh,
Beneath the quilts, the dreams reply.
In winter's arms, we softly drift,
Through the magic of a snowy gift.

Chasing shadows in fading light,
Lost in wonder, everything's bright.
The fire crackles, warmth in the air,
In dreams of winter, we find care.

The world outside wears a silvery crown,
With every heartbeat, the whirl slows down.
In this realm where memories blend,
Time freezes, yet hearts can mend.

Painting visions with frosted breath,
Exploring life, conquering death.
In this dreamland, we hold tight,
To the beauty of winter's night.

Frosted Emotions

A heart encased in a crystal shell,
Whispers of warmth amidst the swell.
Frozen tears that glimmer bright,
Finding solace in the night.

Each heartbeat slow, like falling snow,
In the chill, our true selves show.
Emotions layered, thick with frost,
In solitude, we find what's lost.

Branches bow with burdens of ice,
Carrying stories, chillingly nice.
The world outside feels far away,
In this stillness, we learn to stay.

Frosted windows, a frame of thoughts,
Revealing battles that time forgot.
Through the cold, our spirits rise,
In winter's grasp, love never dies.

The Calmness of Chilled Air

A stillness fills the evening sky,
Gentle whispers of the night breeze,
Breath of winter as it passes by,
Wrapped in warmth, nature's quiet tease.

With frost upon the frozen ground,
Every step leaves a trace behind,
In this serenity, peace is found,
A moment pure, the heart aligned.

Stars appear like distant flames,
Glowing softly, a celestial show,
While the world, beneath their claims,
Stays in slumber, safe from snow.

The trees wear coats of silver white,
Glittering under the moon's soft gaze,
Nature rests before the light,
In the stillness, time delays.

In chilled air, dreams take flight,
Wrapped in silence, dreams draw near,
The calmness of the frozen night,
Fills the soul with quiet cheer.

Dances of Ice and Light

Crystals spark in morning's glow,
Gliding soft on frosty streams,
Nature's dance in a wintry show,
A ballet spun from snowflakes' dreams.

Sunrise paints with golden hues,
Each flake twirls in light's embrace,
A symphony of blues and views,
Ice and warmth share a fleeting space.

Whispers weave through the cold air,
As shadows stretch across the ground,
In this dance, all hearts will share,
The quiet beauty that's found around.

Branches bow with heavy grace,
Holding secrets of winter's art,
In the still, there's a bright trace,
Of joy that warms the chilly heart.

Every shimmer tells a tale,
Of moments caught in frozen time,
Where ice and light, they never fail,
To blend in rhythms, soft and prime.

Reflections in Snow

Stillness blankets all around,
A white canvas beneath the skies,
Echoes of silence softly found,
In the snow, the world complies.

Mirrored thoughts in fallen flakes,
Each one unique, a fleeting sign,
Gathered whispers, winter breaks,
On this snow, our dreams align.

Footprints trace a journey new,
Each step reveals a path we take,
In the quiet, thoughts break through,
Reflections dance, for wonder's sake.

Branches heavy, cloaked in white,
Casting shadows on the ground,
Underneath the pale moonlight,
Reflections of the night abound.

Embraced by this tranquil scene,
Hearts entwined in frosty bliss,
Nature's tranquil, pure routine,
In each soft flake, a gentle kiss.

The Soft Sound of Crystal

Frosty breezes weave their tune,
Crystals chime on branches high,
Echoing softly, like a rune,
Nature sings beneath the sky.

Whispers linger in the air,
As winter's breath creates the sound,
A melody both sweet and rare,
In this silence, peace is found.

Footfalls hush on snowy ground,
Every step a note composed,
In this moment, magic bound,
The soft sound of winter, enclosed.

Tinkling laughter fills the night,
As stars above begin to play,
In the hush, there's pure delight,
Every crystal finds a way.

Listen close, and you may hear,
The songs of chilled and crystal air,
In the softness, warmth draws near,
Life's sweet music everywhere.

The Beauty of Silent Nights

Stars glimmer softly in the dark,
A hush blankets the world, a tranquil spark.
Moonlight dances on the frozen ground,
In this stillness, pure magic is found.

Whispers of frost greet the silver trees,
Carrying secrets on a gentle breeze.
As shadows stretch and the hour grows late,
The heart finds solace, the soul feels great.

Crickets have quieted their evening song,
In the silence, we feel we belong.
A landscape wrapped in a crystal veil,
In this night's embrace, dreams shall prevail.

With every heartbeat, the night unfolds,
In the chill, warmth of memories holds.
Awake to wonder beneath starlit skies,
In the beauty of silence, our spirit flies.

So let us cherish these moments rare,
As beauty lingers in the cold night air.
For in the stillness, we find our way,
Embraced by night until the break of day.

Glacial Reveries

In the cradle of winter, dreams arise,
Glacial peaks touch the indigo skies.
Rippling streams freeze in quiet repose,
Nature whispers softly as stillness grows.

Cotton clouds weave through the air so light,
Draping the world in a soft white sight.
Frosted branches shimmer with each breath,
While nature holds us close as if in death.

The horizon blushes in hues of gold,
Each moment captured, a story told.
Winds carry laughter of days gone by,
Beneath the vastness where eagles fly.

Silhouettes dance through the crystalline night,
Casting shadows that flicker with light.
In reveries deep, our thoughts take flight,
In glacial splendor, everything feels right.

So let us wander where the ice glows bright,
Entranced by the chill, our hearts ignite.
For in this still moment, we embrace the past,
In glacial reveries, love is steadfast.

Where the Cold Embraces

In the heart of winter, where the cold embraces,
Nature pauses, revealing hidden places.
Snowflakes flutter like whispers divine,
Each flake unique, a sparkling design.

Mountain ranges wear their crystal gowns,
Beneath the moonlight, they sigh and frown.
Silence blankets the world, so profound,
In the quiet, such grace can be found.

Branches bend under the weight of the snow,
A path leads us forth, as soft winds blow.
Footprints trail where the shadows play,
Carried along by the night's gentle sway.

The moon casts shadows, a soft silver hue,
Illuminating dreams while the night is new.
In the stillness, we hear our hearts sing,
In the cold embrace, warmth becomes a thing.

Let us linger where silence speaks loud,
In the arms of winter, under nature's shroud.
For when the cold embraces, we come alive,
In this frozen sanctum, our spirits thrive.

In the Arms of Winter's Peace

Snowflakes whisper secrets to the ground,
In soft winter's arms, tranquility is found.
Each breath of chill fills the heart with ease,
In this moment, we find sweet release.

Icicles dangle like delicate dreams,
Cascading light in the sun's soft beams.
The world pauses, caught in pure bliss,
Each second in time, a tender kiss.

Beneath the frost, life quietly waits,
In nature's embrace, we open the gates.
A canvas of white, so pure and bright,
In winter's peace, everything feels right.

With every star that twinkles above,
The night wraps us close with gentle love.
In the silence, a beauty so grand,
In the arms of winter, together we stand.

So let us cherish these moments we share,
In the peace of winter, a love laid bare.
For in each breath of this crisp, cool air,
We find our haven, a space rare and fair.

Serenity in White

The snowflakes dance and twirl,
A blanket soft and bright.
Wrapped in pure tranquility,
Embracing winter's light.

Trees adorned with silken white,
Whispers fill the air.
Footsteps crunch on frozen ground,
A moment free from care.

In the hush, a quiet sigh,
Nature's soothing balm.
Every breath a winter gift,
Awakening the calm.

Glowing lanterns flicker soft,
Guiding through the night.
In this realm of peace, I find
My heart's serene delight.

As stars peek through the veil,
Each glimmer sparks a thought.
Serenity in white enfolds,
In dreams, I've surely caught.

Frozen Dreams

In icy realms where silence dwells,
The world is wrapped in dreams.
Each breath is smoke, a fleeting ghost,
In glistening, silver beams.

The river flows yet stands so still,
Beneath a glassy sheet.
Reflections of a brittle sky,
Where earth and heavens meet.

Crystal branches arch above,
Like chandeliers of ice.
Every flake a whispered wish,
In winter's soft embrace.

Through frozen fields, I wander wide,
In search of hidden grace.
With every step, a dream anew,
A memory to trace.

The landscape breathes, a world asleep,
In slumber's gentle sway.
Frozen dreams of yesteryears,
Will thaw with coming day.

The Calm After the Flurry

The storm has passed, tranquility reigns,
All is hushed and still.
A fresh, white world from chaos born,
Embracing winter's chill.

Each rooftop dons a velvet coat,
While shadows gently creep.
The air is crisp, a gentle kiss,
Awakening from sleep.

In gardens where the wild winds howled,
The world now seems at peace.
With every breath, the beauty grows,
In moments that don't cease.

Birds return, their songs revived,
As sunbeams start to play.
The calm after the flurry sings,
Of brighter, warmer days.

In this stillness, hope ignites,
A promise in the snow.
The calm brings forth a gentle heart,
To cherish all we know.

Chasing Winter's Breath

Through frosty trails, I wander far,
With every crunch beneath.
The winter's breath, a dance of frost,
A chill that feels like peace.

I chase the whispers on the breeze,
Where shadows gently play.
The world adorned in icy lace,
In twilight's soft array.

The mountains loom, a guardian's gaze,
Beneath the silver skies.
Each step echoes winter's song,
Where beauty never lies.

Moments freeze like captured dreams,
In this enchanted sphere.
Chasing winter's breath tonight,
I find my spirit here.

As dawn unveils a pastel glow,
The magic lingers yet.
Chasing what the heart can hold,
In every breath, I let.

Elysium of the Icy Realm

In a world of glistening white,
Shadows dance under pale moonlight.
Frost-kissed trees stand tall and proud,
Their silence speaks beneath the cloud.

Crystal rivers gently flow,
Where secrets of winter softly glow.
Nature's quilt, a serene embrace,
In this ethereal, frozen space.

Whispers of ice, a chilling breeze,
Carried through the ancient trees.
Time stands still, a frozen dream,
In the heart of this icy theme.

Stars above, like diamonds bright,
Guard this realm throughout the night.
Echoes of peace, the world in blue,
Elysium calls, and I follow through.

Every breath, a cloud of mist,
In this paradise, none can resist.
Elysium lives in every flake,
In the icy realm, where hearts awake.

The Geometry of Frost

Shapes and angles carved in ice,
Nature's art, both warm and nice.
Patterns weave through every breath,
A tapestry of life and death.

In the stillness, a crystal sigh,
Formations rise, reaching high.
Symmetry in chilly delight,
Frosted edges sharp and bright.

Circles form in twilight's grace,
Echoes dance in quiet space.
Geometry whispers in the air,
With frozen tales beyond compare.

Every flake, a masterpiece,
A fleeting moment that won't cease.
In the cold, a beauty vast,
The geometry of frost holds fast.

Across the world, in silent flight,
Frost patterns greet the coming night.
A language spoken clear and true,
In shapes of white, the world anew.

Weightless Whispers of Winter

Softly falls the gentle snow,
Weightless whispers, ebb and flow.
Each flake, a story yet untold,
In sparkling white, a world unfolds.

Through the hush of winter's breath,
Nature sighs, a dance with death.
In quietude, the heart takes flight,
With weightless whispers of the night.

Frozen dreams, like stars above,
Carried on the wings of love.
In the stillness, time stands still,
Weightless whispers, a heart to fill.

Beneath the canopy of gray,
Winter's charm will gently play.
Each gust of wind, a tender song,
In this ballet where we belong.

Winter's breath, a fleeting kiss,
In every flake, a taste of bliss.
Weightless whispers in the air,
Guide us through this frozen affair.

The Stillness of Falling Light

As daylight fades, the shadows grow,
A luminescence starts to show.
In twilight's arms, the world finds peace,
The stillness of falling light, a sweet release.

Golden hues give way to gray,
As evening whispers, "Come, let's stay."
Softly fades the vibrant sight,
In the calm of approaching night.

Crickets sing their nighttime tune,
Beneath the watchful, silver moon.
Stars awaken, the sky ignites,
In the stillness of falling light.

Each moment held in twilight's grasp,
A gentle warmth, a tender clasp.
As shadows merge, the world seems right,
In the stillness of falling light.

Every sigh is filled with grace,
In this tranquil, sacred space.
Let the night bring forth our dreams,
In the stillness, life redeems.

Frost-kissed Stillness

In the morn, a quiet sigh,
Whispers from the azure sky.
Each flake falls, a silver gleam,
The world wrapped in a frosty dream.

Branches wear a crystal crown,
Nature sleeps, the day slows down.
The air is crisp, a silent song,
In this stillness, we belong.

Footsteps crunch on frosted ground,
A symphony of whispers found.
As sunlight dances on the ice,
The softest touch, a paradise.

Clouds drift by like thoughts of old,
Secrets in the chill unfold.
In tranquil moments, time stands still,
A heart at peace, a gentle thrill.

A Blanket of Tranquility

Snowflakes weave a gentle shroud,
Covering the earth so proud.
Each patch pure, a serene sight,
Embracing all in soft white light.

Silence wraps the sleeping land,
Nature's touch, a soothing hand.
Hushed tones linger in the air,
A world at peace, beyond compare.

Morning breaks with blush and glow,
Casting warmth on frozen woe.
Beneath this vast, enchanted dome,
Every heart can find a home.

Time flows slow in this embrace,
In every flake, a whispered grace.
Dreams awaken with each gleam,
Wrapped in winter's quiet dream.

Hushed Echoes of Ice

Whispers float on wintry air,
Soft reflections everywhere.
Frozen stillness speaks in hush,
In the heart, a gentle rush.

Icicles hang like crystal tears,
Memories echo through the years.
Each breath forms a frosty plume,
Within the cold, a hidden bloom.

The twilight casts a chilling glow,
As night descends, the stars bestow.
In shadows deep, the silence grows,
A mystery that winter knows.

Beneath the moon's soft, sparkling gaze,
Time pauses in a frozen daze.
With every sigh, a tale unfolds,
Hushed echoes of ice, stories told.

Glimmering in the Chill

The world sparkles, a diamond field,
Every breath a warmth revealed.
In the twilight, shadows play,
Glimmering secrets of the day.

Branches bend with glittering grace,
Nature's charm in icy embrace.
Footprints trace a path of light,
In the evening, calm and bright.

Stars twinkle in the velvet night,
Whispering dreams in pure delight.
Underneath a frosted sky,
Chilled moments gently fly.

Every flake a masterpiece,
Silent beauty that won't cease.
In the cold, we find the thrill,
Life glimmers in the chill.

Frosted Whispers

Whispers ride on chilly winds,
The world adorned in white.
Footsteps crunch on frosted ground,
A tranquil, snowy night.

Moonlight glistens on the trees,
Stars twinkle with delight.
Nature sleeps in icy peace,
Wrapped in soft, pale light.

Shadows dance in winter's mist,
Echoes soft and slow.
Every breath a cloud of steam,
As time begins to slow.

Silent moments, pure and clear,
Hearts find warmth in cold.
In this freeze, the world feels near,
Eternal stories told.

Frosted whispers, sweet and light,
Embrace the world so wide.
In winter's stillness, hearts take flight,
As dreams begin to glide.

Winter's Gentle Embrace

Snowflakes drift from skies above,
A blanket soft and warm.
Nature cradles all within,
In winter's tranquil charm.

Bare branches reach for heavens high,
As frost designs its art.
Whispers of the cold wind sigh,
A soothing, icy heart.

Gentle streams flow slow and deep,
With time, it ebbs and flows.
In this stillness, secrets keep,
Where snow and silence grows.

Luminous dusk meets dawn's soft glow,
A dance of white and gray.
In winter's arms, love starts to grow,
And warms the coldest day.

Through snowy nights, the world ignites,
With sparkles in the dark.
Winter's grace, a sweet sight,
Leaves whispers in the park.

Crystal Silence

A hush envelops every street,
Where quietude resides.
Crystal silence, pure and sweet,
In twilight, peace abides.

Icicles hang like frozen dreams,
Their beauty sharp and clear.
The world, it glimmers, gently beams,
Holding magic near.

Footsteps echo in the night,
As shadows softly blend.
Moonlit paths reveal the light,
Where silence finds a friend.

Stars above in velvet space,
Softly wink in delight.
In crystal silence, time finds grace,
Embodying the night's flight.

The heart beats slow, the mind is free,
In stillness, dreams unite.
Crystal silence, harmony,
Embraces souls in flight.

Beneath the Silver Veil

Underneath the silver veil,
Where shadows softly play,
Frozen whispers gently sail,
Upon the world at bay.

Branches bow, their burden strong,
With snowflakes, softly light,
Nature sings a haunting song,
In this enchanted night.

Footprints trace a quiet path,
Through woods of frosted lace.
In the stillness, hearts can laugh,
Finding warmth in this space.

Stars adorn the night like dreams,
While cold wraps all around.
Beneath the silver veil, it seems,
Magic can be found.

Holding hands, hearts pulse as one,
In moments soft and rare.
Beneath the silver veil, we run,
Embraced by winter's air.

Soft Footfalls on a Crystal Canvas

Whispers of snow beneath my feet,
A world aglow, where silence meets.
Each step a dance, a fleeting grace,
Nature's art, a tranquil space.

Leaves of frost adorn the trees,
Glistening softly in the breeze.
A canvas pure, so vast and wide,
Where peace and stillness now reside.

Footprints trace a path unseen,
Through shimmering fields of frozen sheen.
With every breath, the air so clear,
A sparkling world, I hold so dear.

The sky above, a muted hue,
Reflects the dreams I thought I knew.
In quiet wonder, I explore,
This crystal land forevermore.

As daylight fades, the stars ignite,
With whispers soft, embracing night.
In this realm of frost and glow,
Each footfall sings, a tale of snow.

Veils of White in Shimmering Light

Veils of white, a soft embrace,
Blanket the world in gentle lace.
Morning rays in tender play,
Illuminate the snowy gray.

Trees adorned in silver hue,
Draped in whispers, pure and true.
Every branch a jeweled crown,
In sparkling grace, they won't back down.

Through quiet paths, my heart does roam,
In frozen realms, I've found my home.
Each flake that falls a fleeting dance,
In nature's grasp, I take a chance.

The crunch of snow beneath my feet,
A symphony, so bright, so sweet.
As twilight paints the sky with gold,
A story new begins to unfold.

Stars emerge in velvet skies,
As frosted dreams begin to rise.
In every breath, a world of light,
Veils of white embrace the night.

A Tapestry of Icicles and Silence

Icicles hang like crystal spears,
A tapestry that time endears.
Silent whispers fill the air,
In nature's charm, there's room to share.

The world adorned in icy threads,
Sparkling where the sunlight spreads.
A wondrous sight, a fleeting grace,
Each drop a moment to embrace.

Amidst the chill, the heart beats strong,
In stillness where the dreams belong.
A quiet trust in winter's might,
Wraps the world in pure delight.

Each breath a cloud, a secret mist,
In this embrace, I can't resist.
A dance of flakes on gentle wings,
In silence deep, a heartbeat sings.

With every glance, a story's spun,
Of winter's grace, of love begun.
A tapestry of life in bloom,
Where icicles declare their room.

Frost-Kissed Moments in Time

Frost-kissed mornings, cool and bright,
A canvas painted, pure delight.
With every breath, the world awakes,
In gentle hush, the silence breaks.

Each crystal flake, a fleeting thought,
In winter's grasp, our dreams are caught.
Moments linger, soft and sweet,
In frosty air, my heart's retreat.

Sunshine glimmers on the ice,
Nature's beauty, a jeweled slice.
The whispering winds weave through the trees,
Carrying secrets on the breeze.

Frozen lakes like mirrors stand,
Reflecting skies, a painted land.
In each soft touch of winter's hand,
Life's gentle rhythm, slowly planned.

As daylight wanes, the shadows play,
Crafting stories in shades of gray.
Frost-kissed moments linger on,
In winter's arms, I feel so strong.

Frosted Dreams Take Flight

In twilight glow, dreams arise,
Softly dancing in the skies.
Wings of white in a gentle breeze,
Carried far with graceful ease.

Snowflakes whisper secrets sweet,
A world transformed beneath their feet.
Each soft flake a fleeting thought,
In frozen moments, hope is sought.

Laughter strains like silver threads,
Beneath the moon where stillness spreads.
Hearts afloat in winter's hand,
In frosted realms, together we stand.

Let the chill embrace us tight,
As dreams take wing into the night.
Gentle shadows come to play,
In the stillness of the day.

In every breath, a spark ignites,
As dreams take flight on crystal nights.
Boundless skies invite the soul,
To chase the warmth and feel whole.

Silence Beneath the White Veil

A blanket falls, soft as a sigh,
Quiet whispers as winter draws nigh.
Beneath the veil of white so pure,
Silence lingers, calm and sure.

Frosted branches, a sparkling guise,
Glistening gently like the stars in the skies.
Nature holds its breath, so still,
As snowflakes dance upon the hill.

Footsteps muffled, all is at rest,
In this realm, the heart feels blessed.
Each flake tells a story anew,
Of tranquil moments and morning dew.

The world transformed, a wondrous sight,
In softest hues of silver light.
Beneath the white veil lies a dream,
Where silence reigns and peace does gleam.

In this cocoon, worries drift away,
As winter's hush holds sway.
Embrace the stillness, feel the calm,
In the frost, we find our balm.

Quietude in the Crystal Lattice

Amidst the woods, a still expanse,
Where shadows play and chill can dance.
Intricate patterns, nature's art,
A crystal lattice, calm at heart.

Each branch adorned in frozen lace,
Holds the whispers of a secret place.
Gentle winds weave through the trees,
A symphony played with winter's keys.

In this haven, time suspends,
A quietude that softly mends.
Every breath a fragile note,
In this haven, souls can float.

Imprints linger in the snow,
Stories of journeys, tales to show.
With every step, a new delight,
In the crystal lattice, pure and bright.

Let serenity guide our way,
Through hidden paths of cold and gray.
In stillness find our hearts align,
Within this beauty, we will shine.

The Stillness of a Frozen Whisper

In the quiet, a whisper calls,
Soft as winter's gentle thralls.
Frozen breath hangs in the air,
A stillness lingers everywhere.

Snowflakes tumble, a tender song,
Nature hums where we belong.
In every flake, a story's breath,
Of life, of love, in gentle death.

Crystals form on every bough,
Silent moments live right now.
A hush that blankets night and day,
In this tranquility, dreams can play.

The world lies wrapped in white embrace,
Finding peace in this still space.
In frozen whispers, secrets flow,
As time stands still beneath the snow.

Let us wander through this peace,
As moments blend and sorrows cease.
In the stillness, hearts align,
In frozen whispers, we will shine.

Melodies on a Snow-Covered Path

Whispers of snow beneath our feet,
A symphony soft, a winter's greet.
Pine trees dressed in frosted white,
Guiding us through the gentle night.

Branches bow low with crystal lace,
Each step taken, a fleeting trace.
The silence sings, a tranquil song,
In this wonderland, we belong.

Footprints linger, then fade away,
In the dusky light of the day.
Moonlit shadows dance on ground,
In the stillness, magic is found.

Echoes of joy in frosty air,
Moments cherished, beyond compare.
Together we roam, hand in hand,
On this snow-covered, dreamlike land.

As melodies drift, hearts beat as one,
In the realm of ice, our journey begun.
With every breath, we weave a tale,
Of love and warmth in a wintry veil.

Luminescence in the Frostbitten Air

Stars twinkle bright in the frigid night,
Shimmering whispers, a magical sight.
Frost crystals sparkle on the ground,
In the stillness, beauty is found.

The moon casts shadows that softly gleam,
A world transformed, like a dream.
Cold winds murmur through the trees,
Carrying secrets on the breeze.

Every breath shows a frosty mist,
As we wander without a tryst.
Nature's canvas, painted so bright,
Illuminating the heart of the night.

Wonders of winter in every face,
In this chill, we find our place.
Together we laugh, we dance, we play,
In the glowing night, we drift away.

Luminescence guides our way home,
Through the frost, no need to roam.
In the warmth of love, we find our glow,
In a world that sparkles with winter's show.

Flickering Embers Against the Chill

By the fire's warmth, we gather near,
Flickering embers cut through the fear.
With every crackle, stories unfold,
In the glow of night, our hearts turned bold.

Outside the wind, a howling song,
But inside here, we can't go wrong.
Hot cocoa steaming, laughter bright,
As we chase away the winter's bite.

Blankets wrapped tight, comfort we crave,
In the hearth's glow, we feel so brave.
Whispers of love fill the air,
As we cherish moments beyond compare.

Crimson flames dance, shadows waltz,
Each ember speaks, without a false.
In the depth of night, we hold each other,
Finding warmth like no other.

As stars twinkle through the icy pane,
Together we weather the night's domain.
With flickering flames our spirits rise,
In this cocoon, the world feels wise.

The Winter's Lullaby

The world in white, softly asleep,
Winter's lullaby, a promise to keep.
Snowflakes flutter, twirling around,
In gentle whispers, peace is found.

Branches swaying in the nighttime breeze,
Carving out dreams with effortless ease.
Each sparkle glistens under the moon,
A soft serenade, a winter's tune.

Crimson skies fade into deep blues,
While night blankets the earth with its cues.
In the hush, nature's heart does sigh,
With every breath, the world draws nigh.

Cuddle in warmth, let the coldness pass,
In this quiet, let worries amass.
A cradle of snow shields our hearts,
As whispers of winter sweetly imparts.

The stars above keep watchful eyes,
As dreams take flight, under winter skies.
The world may freeze, yet love will flow,
In winter's embrace, watch our hearts grow.

Beneath the Flakes of Time

Beneath the flakes that softly fall,
Whispers of history softly call.
Each flake a memory, frozen bright,
Dancing softly in the pale moonlight.

In quiet moments, the world stands still,
Nature pauses, wrapped in a chill.
Silence blankets all with gentle grace,
As time unfurls in this hallowed space.

The trees wear coats of sparkling white,
Branches adorned, a stunning sight.
Footprints trace where dreams have been,
Stories linger in the frost's sheen.

In the stillness, feelings arise,
Like distant echoes from the skies.
Life's journey, through seasons, flows,
Beneath the flakes, the heart still knows.

Tranquil Hues of Winter's Breath

In the hush of winter's breath,
Colors blend in a peaceful wreath.
Whites and blues swirl in the air,
Nature's canvas, beautifully rare.

The sun dips low, a golden ray,
Casting warmth at the close of day.
Soft shadows stretch across the land,
Winter's solstice, quiet and grand.

Crisp air fills the lungs, so clear,
Each moment savored, held dear.
Footsteps crunch on a frosted trail,
With every breath, winter's tale.

Icicles glisten like hanging gems,
Nature's art, no need for hems.
Life slows down in the chilly mist,
A tranquil scene that can't be missed.

Embrace the chill, the world transforms,
Winter's peace in all its forms.
In tranquil hues, we find our place,
A gentle refuge, a warm embrace.

The Elegy of a Frozen Morning

The frozen morning greets the dawn,
A shimmering veil on the lawn.
Whispers of frost cling to the grass,
Silent stories as moments pass.

In the stillness, dreams reside,
Beneath the snow, where secrets hide.
Each breath a cloud, a fleeting sigh,
Time stands still beneath the sky.

Nature's palette, white and gray,
Colors muted in the light of day.
A quiet elegy hums along,
As winter sings its gentle song.

Branch and bough, in frozen lace,
Adorned with crystals, a soft embrace.
The world awakens from its night,
Meeting the morning's fragile light.

In the elegance of icy breath,
Lies a beauty that conquers death.
Moments captured in frosty art,
Echoes of winter, close to the heart.

Winter's Gentle Invitation

Winter's whisper calls us near,
In frosted air, the vision's clear.
Pines stand tall, a silent choir,
Wrapping the world in softest fire.

Each flake that falls, a tender kiss,
An invitation to blissful bliss.
Hot cocoa warms the chilly hands,
As laughter dances across the lands.

Every breath, a frosty plume,
Icicles hang like crystal bloom.
Snowflakes twirl in a playful dance,
Nature's call, a twinkling chance.

Gather 'round as the twilight glows,
In winter's embrace, the spirit flows.
Gentle moments, a sweet refrain,
In winter's arms, we feel no pain.

With every heartbeat, the world turns white,
A sacred space, where day meets night.
Winter beckons with open hands,
Inviting all to make their plans.

Serenity Wrapped in Frost

Amidst the silent, whispering trees,
A blanket of white hugs the earth's knees.
Crystals gleam as the dawn breaks bright,
Winter's embrace, a pure, gentle light.

Footprints crunch on the frosty ground,
In the hush of the world, peace is found.
Breath rises like fog in the crisp air,
Moments like these teach us to care.

The sun peeks over the shadowed hills,
Casting warmth through the cold, it instills.
Sparks of joy dance in the winter glow,
Where time slows down and hope starts to grow.

A soft breeze carries the scent of pine,
Nature's artwork in tangled design.
Serenity whispers, the world is still,
Wrapped in frost, with time to fulfill.

Snowflakes twirl, a delicate dance,
Each one unique, a breath of chance.
In this moment, worries are lost,
In the beauty of winter, we count the cost.

Midnight Snowfall Serenade

Under the blanket of night so deep,
Snowflakes flutter, the world in sleep.
Softly they land with a tender grace,
Carpeting silence in this sacred space.

Moonlight kisses the shimmering snow,
Whispers of winter, a gentle flow.
Each flake a note in a lullaby,
Sung to the stars in the inky sky.

Branches bow under the softest weight,
Nature's embrace, a serene fate.
Time pauses as the world holds its breath,
In the stillness, we dance with death.

Midnight's magic, a soothing balm,
Warmth of the hearth, a sacred calm.
The frost-laden air sparkles with cheer,
Echoes of dreams that we hold dear.

With each falling flake, a wish is made,
In the quiet night, worries fade.
A serenade sung by the winter's choir,
Wrapping us in its gentle fire.

The Heart's Hearth in Chill

As the cold wind whispers through the trees,
We gather close, hearts find their ease.
The fire crackles, stories unfold,
In the warmth of the hearth, love is bold.

Cocoa in hand, we share our tales,
Embers glow while the night unveils.
In tempest's grasp, we stand as one,
Finding comfort till the dark is done.

Frosted windows frame our laughter's glow,
Inside, our memories steadily flow.
The chill may bite, but we hold tight,
In this haven, everything feels right.

Outside the world wears a frosty guise,
But in our hearts, summer never dies.
The hearth's gentle warmth, a soothing balm,
In every heartbeat, we find our calm.

So let the cold rage and winds howl,
Within these walls, love we avow.
In the heart's hearth, our spirits thrill,
Together forever, we conquer the chill.

Reflections in a Winter's Mirror

Glistening surfaces reflect the night,
The world transformed in silver light.
Frozen lakes bear the weight of dreams,
Tranquil beauty, or so it seems.

Peering close, the stories unfold,
Waves of winter, rich and bold.
Each ripple a whisper of the past,
Frozen memories, too precious to last.

The pines stand tall, their crowns aglow,
As winter echoes secrets below.
In stillness, reflections reveal,
The heart's wish wrapped in the wheel.

As hours glide in the chilling embrace,
We ponder the heart's most sacred place.
In the mirror of ice, we see what's true,
Illuminated by the cold's soft hue.

Winter's mirror, both fierce and clear,
Reminds us of all that we hold dear.
In every glance, life's fleeting grace,
We'll treasure the warmth in this cold space.

The Magic of Crystal Clarity

In the morn, the light breaks free,
Casting shadows, a whispered plea.
Crystals form on branches high,
Nature's spell beneath the sky.

Each drop glimmers like a star,
Reflecting dreams from near and far.
In silence, truths begin to show,
In crystal clarity, we glow.

Beneath the frosted canopy,
Lies a world of harmony.
Echoing through the stillness bright,
The magic dances in the light.

In the shimmering, frozen air,
Beauty whispers everywhere.
A moment caught, so pure, so rare,
In the magic, we'll always share.

As we wander through this realm,
Feel the peace, let love overwhelm.
For in the cold, our spirits soar,
Crystal clarity opens the door.

Hibernation of the Heart

In the stillness, shadows play,
Dreams retreat, hiding away.
Softly winter's breath does call,
Encasing hopes in a tender thrall.

Beneath the snow, the heart does rest,
Wrapped in silence, nature's vest.
Through the cold, warmth often hides,
Yearning for spring's gentle tides.

In this pause, reflections grow,
Memories drift, like falling snow.
Time suspends in quiet grace,
As shadows dance in this safe place.

Through the dark, we find our way,
In each night, there comes a day.
Hope is buried, but not lost,
In hibernation, love pays the cost.

When the thaw begins to tease,
Life emerges with tender ease.
Hearts awake, the world ignites,
In hibernation, we find our sights.

Serenity Found in Frost

Morning breaks with icy grace,
Frosted whispers in their place.
Chill of night meets sun's warm smile,
Nature's beauty, pause awhile.

Each branch drapes a crystal shawl,
Serenity in nature's thrall.
Frozen leaves in silver glow,
A tranquil scene, a gentle flow.

In the hush, a moment shared,
Frosted dreams that nature dared.
Whispers soft, as breezes weave,
In this calm, we learn to believe.

Life slows down in winter's hold,
Stories whispered, yet untold.
In the stillness, hearts connect,
Serenity that we protect.

Underneath the frosty veil,
Peaceful echoes gently sail.
In winter's grip, we find our rest,
Serenity, at its very best.

Chasing the Winter Whisper

On the breeze, soft secrets fly,
Whispers dance, fading nigh.
Chasing echoes, we pursue,
The songs that winter sings anew.

Through the fields, with crystal light,
Winter wears its attire bright.
Each sound carries tales untold,
In every flake, a story bold.

Quiet moments, hearts take flight,
Chasing whispers into night.
Footsteps crunch on frozen ground,
In this stillness, joy is found.

Frosty air, a breath so clear,
Whispers beckon, drawing near.
Nestled close, we share the thrill,
Of winter's voice, a silent chill.

So we wander, hand in hand,
Chasing dreams across the land.
With each whisper, magic flows,
In winter's heart, our spirit glows.

Beneath the Winter Sky

Beneath the winter sky, so wide,
The stars begin to gleam and glide.
Snowflakes dance on a frosty breeze,
Whispers carry through the trees.

Moonlight drapes on frozen ground,
In silence, only peace is found.
The world is wrapped in a silver veil,
As winter's song begins to sail.

Footprints trace a path so clear,
Echoes of laughter, warm and near.
Children's joy in the crisp, cold air,
Dreams take flight, without a care.

Fires crackle in homes so bright,
Bringing warmth on this winter night.
Love and laughter softly blend,
A cozy hearth, where hearts can mend.

Beneath the winter sky we stand,
Holding dreams in a tender hand.
With every star that twinkles high,
We find our peace beneath the sky.

Lullabies of the Frost

The night descends, a blanket white,
Lullabies of frost take flight.
Softly whispers, a soothing sound,
In the stillness, peace is found.

Crystals twinkle in moon's embrace,
Every shadow finds its place.
Gentle breaths of winter's air,
Wrap the world in calm and care.

Snowflakes fall, like dreams they drift,
Nature's lullaby, a precious gift.
Branches bow with a tender sigh,
As winter whispers softly by.

Fires flicker, shadows play,
In cozy nooks, we wish to stay.
Hot cocoa warms our chilly hands,
While outside, the quiet lands.

In this realm of frosted dreams,
Life is sweet as it gently seems.
Wrapped in winter's soft embrace,
We find our home, our sacred place.

Veil of Winter's Magic

Veil of winter's magic strong,
We gather close, we sing our song.
With every note, our voices blend,
In harmony, our hearts transcend.

Frosted branches, bright and fair,
Glisten softly, in chilled air.
Every flake an artist's touch,
Painting landscapes, oh so much.

In the quiet, dreams take flight,
Wrapped in warmth of gentle light.
Stars above seem to wink and nod,
In this wonder, we find God.

Candles flicker, shadows twist,
In this moment, we can't resist.
Hot fires crackle, love surrounds,
In winter's joy, our laughter sounds.

Beneath the sky of silvery hue,
We find the magic, pure and true.
In frosted wonder, hearts align,
Veil of winter, forever divine.

In the Heart of Winter

In the heart of winter's chill,
Quiet whispers make us still.
Nature sleeps beneath the frost,
In this peace, we find the lost.

Footprints trace on paths anew,
In the snow, a world askew.
Memories wrapped in layers white,
Twinkling stars adorn the night.

Hot tea steams in the evening glow,
While outside, the cold winds blow.
Through the windows, we see the glow,
Of flickering flames, our hearts aglow.

Together gathered, hand in hand,
In this winter wonderland.
Stories told by shadows cast,
In the heart of winter, we hold fast.

As daylight fades, the night draws near,
In the silence, we feel no fear.
For in this season, our spirits play,
In the heart of winter, we find our way.

Enchanted by the Cold

Whispers in the icy air,
Trees adorned in frosty flair,
Moonlight dances on the snow,
Magic sparkles, soft and low.

Crisp and clear, the night unfolds,
A world in silver, bright and bold,
Footsteps crunch on chilly ground,
In this stillness, peace is found.

Stars above, in silence gleam,
Frozen moments like a dream,
Every breath a cloud of white,
Lost in wonder, pure delight.

Branches draped in glistening lace,
Nature's beauty, a sacred space,
As breath comes forth in frosty puffs,
The cold embraces, gentle, tough.

Enchanted hearts, together thrum,
In winter's hand, the magic comes,
A symphony of chill and grace,
Together here, in this embrace.

A World Wrapped in White

A blanket thick, so soft and deep,
The world transformed, while others sleep,
Hushed are sounds of city play,
In white cocoon, the noise fades away.

Glistening fields of purest hue,
Under skies of gray and blue,
Children's laughter fills the air,
A world wrapped in white, beyond compare.

Snowflakes twirl like fairy dust,
Covering the earth, a sacred trust,
Footprints lead to dreams unknown,
In this realm, we are not alone.

Every twig and branch now dressed,
Nature pauses, takes a rest,
Time stands still, each moment bright,
In this reverie of endless white.

A world awash in tranquil light,
Every shadow lost to night,
We wander through this canvas vast,
In awe of winter's gentle cast.

The Breath of Frost

In the dawn, the breath of frost,
Weaves its patterns, never lost,
Softly brushing every pane,
A tranquil beauty, pure and plain.

Whispers linger in the chill,
Nature's quiet, peaceful will,
Every exhale paints the air,
A fleeting art, beyond compare.

Icicles hang like crystal tears,
Marking time through winter years,
Each sparkle tells a story clear,
Of every moment held so dear.

In this stillness, thoughts take flight,
Wrapped in warmth, igniting light,
The breath of frost, a gentle song,
Inviting us to sing along.

With each step on frosted ground,
Whispers echo all around,
In the quiet, hearts find peace,
As the breath of frost will cease.

Quietude Amongst the Flurries

In gentle dances, flakes descend,
Whirling softly, where paths blend,
A hush envelops, calm and bright,
Quietude reigns in the fading light.

Each flurry tells a tale anew,
Whispering secrets, soft and true,
In the stillness, we take pause,
In wonderment, we find our cause.

Snow-laden boughs sway with grace,
Nature's artistry, a warm embrace,
In the quiet, we breathe deep,
Amongst the flurries, dreams we keep.

Children play in winter's arms,
Building snowmen, sharing charms,
Laughter rings like bells in snow,
In this quietude, love will grow.

As night descends, the world glows bright,
Stars peek through, a dazzling sight,
In the tranquility, hearts align,
Amongst the flurries, all is divine.

Memories Wrapped in Ice

In winter's grasp, we drift and slide,
Moments frozen, time won't bide.
Whispers echo in the cold night air,
Each thought a shadow, light and rare.

Laughter lingers like frost on trees,
Embraced by memories, we feel the freeze.
A world preserved, in silence it stays,
Capturing us in forgotten ways.

Glassy paths where we used to roam,
Winding back to our childhood home.
Fleeting glimpses of joy's sweet trace,
Locked forever in this frozen space.

Yet underneath, the warmth does glow,
Hope embedded beneath the snow.
A spark ignites the chilling night,
Our hearts beat softly, ready to fight.

When spring awakens the icy shroud,
Memories melt, but we are proud.
For in the heart, they shall reside,
Forever cherished, never to hide.

Crystal Pavement

Under the moon, the world shines bright,
Each step we take, a dance of light.
A crystal path beneath our feet,
Echoes like whispers, soft and sweet.

The frost paints glimmers on each stone,
Memories carved in ice alone.
With every footfall, history wakes,
A shimmering tale the pavement makes.

Fog wraps around like a tender shawl,
Beneath this beauty, we rise, we fall.
Each frozen moment, a treasure found,
In every silence, the past resounds.

Stars blink overhead, each one a wish,
Craving the warmth of a fleeting kiss.
Through the chill, our hearts do race,
Finding joy in this enchanting place.

As dawn approaches, the ice will break,
Yet the memories linger, for our sake.
A crystal pavement paved with dreams,
In winter's heart, there's more than it seems.

The Embrace of Cold

In the stillness, the cold unfolds,
Wrapping around, a tale retold.
A breath of winter, crisp and clear,
Carrying secrets we hold so dear.

The embrace of cold, so profound and tight,
Filling our souls with silent delight.
Each crystal flake that dances down,
A fleeting kiss from a winter crown.

Branches adorned in shimmering white,
Guarding the dreams of a starry night.
In this cocoon, we find our way,
Lost in the beauty of frosty play.

Fireside warmth calls out our name,
Yet this chill brings us no shame.
For in the cold, we find our grace,
In every breath, in every space.

Embraced by winter's tender hand,
We cherish the magic that takes a stand.
In the cold's allure, we learn to believe,
In the power of stillness, and how to grieve.

Reflections in a Snowglobe

A snowglobe rests upon the shelf,
Capturing moments, a world itself.
Each swirl of snow, a memory spun,
In its glassy heart, we come undone.

Tiny figures dance in frozen bliss,
Chasing the warmth, we long to kiss.
Time stands still in this fleeting dream,
Life encased in a glistening seam.

Turn it gently, watch it glow,
In every flicker, the stories flow.
Captured laughter, we bring to mind,
In this small world, our hearts entwined.

As seasons change, the stories fade,
Yet in that globe, our love is laid.
With every shake, memories collide,
In its embrace, we choose to abide.

Reflections shining, none can sever,
The bonds we forged will last forever.
For even when life's storms conspire,
In the snowglobe's heart, we find the fire.

Shroud of White around the Soul

In the stillness of the night,
A blanket soft and pure,
It wraps the heart in silence,
A tranquil, soothing lure.

Whispers dance on frosted air,
Carried by the moon's embrace,
Embracing dreams with gentle care,
In this enchanting space.

Veils of snow upon the ground,
Where shadows find their place,
Each flake a memory unbound,
A delicate trace.

In this shroud, the spirit breathes,
Finding solace in the white,
Like hope that gently weaves,
Through the fabric of the night.

Awake, yet lost in thought so deep,
As dawn approaches near,
The world stirs from its sleep,
Awash in calm and sheer.

The Sigh of a Cold Dawn

The night retreats, the stars grow dim,
A whisper from the trees,
Frosty breath with a gentle hymn,
Announcing winter's freeze.

Hushed moments linger in the gray,
As shadows start to fade,
The sun peeks through, a shy display,
On frosted glades it played.

Each blade of grass adorned in ice,
Reflects the morning light,
Nature's canvas, pure and nice,
Bathed in hues of white.

A sigh escapes the waking earth,
A promise of a day,
Where warmth and cold find their worth,
In a dance upon the sway.

Soft whispers travel on the breeze,
A mellow tune unfolds,
The dawn is wrapped in subtle ease,
As winter's tale is told.

Interludes in an Icy Chamber

In the heart of winter's grasp,
A chamber cool and bright,
Reflections shimmer, softly clasp,
In the stillness of the night.

Icicles hang like crystal tears,
In silence they suspend,
Each chime recalls the fleeting years,
Time's intricate blend.

A whisper echoes, crystal clear,
Through the frosted, frozen space,
Where dreams may linger, calm and near,
In this enchanted place.

Shadows play upon the walls,
Bathed in cool, pale blue,
Dancing softly as twilight falls,
In swirling shades anew.

A moment's pause, sweet and rare,
In this icy atmosphere,
Where hearts find warmth through cold despair,
And hope begins to steer.

Ethereal Frost on the Petal's Edge

Amidst the flowers, a shimmer glows,
Each petal kissed by night,
The frost a delicate repose,
Caressed by silver light.

A touch of winter's gentle hand,
Embroidered on each bloom,
As nature weaves her crystal strand,
In the silent, starry room.

Each breath a frosty lullaby,
Cradling blooms with grace,
Where softness meets the starlit sky,
In this ethereal space.

Colors fade, yet beauty stays,
In the chill that softly hugs,
A fleeting glance of winter's ways,
In nature's tender snugs.

The petals bear the weight of dreams,
In the twilight's embrace,
With every sigh, a memory beams,
In this enchanted place.

Artistry of the Icebound World

Glittering shards in the morning light,
Nature's canvas, pure and bright.
Each flake falling, a unique design,
Crafted by winter, a gift divine.

Trees adorned in a frosty lace,
Whispering secrets, they embrace.
Paths untraveled, silence profound,
Artistry hidden beneath the ground.

Mountains dressed in glistening white,
Echoes of beauty, pure delight.
A world transformed in quiet grace,
Where time slows down, our hearts embrace.

Rivers frozen in tranquil flow,
Beneath the ice, life starts to grow.
Each breath of wind, a gentle sigh,
In this wonder, we learn to fly.

While twilight whispers a lullaby,
Stars awaken in the ebony sky.
Nature's artwork, a fleeting space,
In the icebound world, we find our place.

Dreamscapes Adrift in White

Clouds of snow drift through the air,
A dreamscape woven with utmost care.
Whispers of winter beckon us near,
To a world where magic is always clear.

Footprints fade on the glistening ground,
In this silence, pure joy is found.
The horizon blurs, a canvas vast,
In white stillness, we dream and cast.

Winds weave tales of forgotten lore,
In soft whispers, they softly implore.
A journey begins in each flake's fall,
Embracing the dreams that winter enthralls.

Boughs break under the shimmering load,
Nature stands still in a quiet code.
Artistry flows in the chill of the night,
Each moment suspended, serene, and bright.

As the moonlight dances on frozen streams,
We wander through the land of dreams.
Each breath we take, a fleeting delight,
In dreamscapes adrift, we take our flight.

Solitude Under the Frosted Sky

A quietude whispers beneath the frost,
In the still of night, nothing is lost.
Stars flicker softly, a distant choir,
Under the frost, our souls conspire.

Moments stretch in the crisp, cold air,
Finding solace, free from despair.
Alone yet whole under this expanse,
In solitude's arms, we find our chance.

Breath rises like mist, a ghostly trace,
In the embrace of winter's grace.
The world is hushed, a sacred domain,
Where solitude blooms, devoid of pain.

Echoes of footsteps on the frozen ground,
A rhythm of peace, a gentle sound.
In the chill lies warmth, a hidden spark,
Guiding us gently through the stark.

As dawn breaks slowly, the shadows shift,
Ember glow ignites, the spirits lift.
In solitude, we've found our way,
Beneath the frost, we learn to stay.

Shadows Cast by Winter's Glow

Fires flicker, casting warmth and light,
As winter's shadows dance in the night.
Echoes of laughter, memories blend,
In this twilight where stories mend.

The trees stand tall, silhouettes stark,
Guardians of secrets in the dark.
Beneath the moon's gentle, watchful eye,
Hope glimmers softly, refusing to die.

Snowflakes swirl in a lazy waltz,
Nature's rhythm, never at fault.
Each whispering breeze carries a tune,
A lullaby sweet, beneath the moon.

Shadows lengthen and memories grow,
In the quiet embrace of winter's glow.
Together we stand, hand in hand,
Creating warmth in this icy land.

As dawn breaks, shadows will recede,
Yet winter's glow plants the seed.
For when night falls and silence is found,
We'll treasure the shadows, love unbound.

Luminance in White

Snowflakes drift on gentle air,
Blanketing the world in care.
Softly whispers in the light,
Graceful, pure, a stunning sight.

Moonbeams dance on icy streams,
Casting silvery, radiant beams.
Innocent glows, a tranquil grace,
A harmony we all embrace.

Footprints lead where shadows fall,
Echoes linger, nature's call.
Each step whispers tales of old,
In the stillness, stories unfold.

Beneath the frost, life sleeps tight,
Awaiting spring's warm, tender light.
With every dawn, the promise grows,
Of vibrant blooms and sunlit shows.

Luminance in every flake,
A gift of beauty, one can't fake.
In this world of shimmering white,
Hope is born in purest light.

A Path Through the Stillness

Amidst the trees, the silence reigns,
Footsteps echo softly, gently wanes.
A path unfolds, serene and clear,
Inviting heart and soul to steer.

Whispers linger in the air,
Nature's secrets, rich and rare.
Leaves gently rustle, a calming tune,
Guiding dreams beneath the moon.

Sunlight trickles through the boughs,
Greeting shadows, making vows.
Each moment savored, time stands still,
In this haven, peace we fill.

Crisp air kisses skin so pale,
As footsteps meld with nature's tale.
Wandering freely, hearts take flight,
Through the stillness, pure delight.

A path of wonder calls us near,
In silence wrapped, we lend an ear.
Together lost in earthy grace,
We find ourselves in nature's embrace.

Frosty Caresses of Nature

Morning glimmers, frost-kissed morn,
Nature's touch, a day reborn.
Crystal lace on every blade,
Beauty wrapped in softest shade.

Winter whispers to the trees,
Rustling gently with the breeze.
Every branch a work of art,
Frosted elegance plays its part.

Patterns etched on windowpanes,
Delicate, like love's refrains.
In this chill, warmth finds its way,
Through the heart, in soft display.

Glistening fields, a silent sigh,
Underneath the vast, gray sky.
Nature's quilt, a precious gift,
In frosty caresses, spirits lift.

Amidst the cold, we find our charm,
In every flake, in nature's calm.
Life goes on, in winter's hold,
Frosty caresses, tales untold.

Celestial White Stillness

In the night, a tranquil glow,
Celestial wonders dance below.
Stars sprinkled on the canvas wide,
A silent sea where dreams confide.

Snow drapes softly on the ground,
In this stillness, peace is found.
Moonlight bathes the world in grace,
Washing over time and space.

Whispers blend with winter's song,
Carried forth where hearts belong.
Every moment, a sacred breath,
Painting life in hues of death.

Beneath the calm, a promise lies,
Of resurrection in the skies.
As stillness blankets earth so white,
Hope awakens in the night.

In every flake, a story spun,
Of bonds and bliss, of hearts as one.
Celestial stillness, pure and bright,
Guides us through the endless night.

The Peace of Winter's Kiss

Snow blankets the silent ground,
Whispers of chill all around.
Trees wear coats of frosted lace,
Nature rests in a serene space.

Candles flicker with warm light,
Hearts are cozy, spirits bright.
Softly falling, flakes descend,
Winter's peace, a gentle friend.

Footprints trace a path so clear,
Echoes of laughter, joy sincere.
In the hush, dreams entwine,
Beneath the stars, our hopes align.

Fires crackle with tales of old,
Memories wrapped in warmth, bold.
In this stillness, time stands still,
A tranquil heart, a peaceful will.

The world slows down, a gentle sigh,
Softly painted 'neath the sky.
In the cold, we find our bliss,
In the magic of winter's kiss.

Soft Embrace of Ice

Crisp air tingles, sweet delight,
Branches sway in silver light.
Every flake, a fleeting kiss,
In the quiet, we find bliss.

Frozen lakes like mirrors gleam,
Reflecting every muted dream.
Skaters glide with elegant grace,
Moving slow, a dance in place.

Icicles hang as nature's art,
A chilling touch that warms the heart.
Surrounded by this frosty hue,
Life feels fresh, serene, anew.

Soft whispers of a winter's night,
Stars twinkle, a wondrous sight.
The world wrapped in a soft embrace,
In the magic of winter's grace.

Dreams are spun with icy threads,
As the warmth of friendship spreads.
In every moment, pure and nice,
In winter's arms, a soft embrace.

Shimmering White Oasis

A glimmering coat, nature's dress,
Snowflakes dance, a gentle caress.
In this oasis, peace is found,
Harmony wrapped all around.

Moonlight twinkles on drifts of white,
Illuminating the stillness of night.
Footprints lead where dreams reside,
In winter's arms, we take pride.

Silent meadows, endless and wide,
A canvas where beauty can't hide.
Each gust of wind sings a tune,
Under the watchful eye of the moon.

The air crisp, a breath of chill,
Moments cherished, hearts fulfilled.
In the quiet, our spirits soar,
In this oasis, forevermore.

Every glance, a postcard scene,
Life feels like a peaceful dream.
In shimmering white, joy's embrace,
Winter's call, a warm grace.

The Quiet Dance of Winter

Softly falls the evening snow,
Whispers of winter, sweet and slow.
Under stars, a world alight,
In the quiet of the night.

Branches bow from the frozen weight,
Nature hushes, it's never late.
A ballet of silence in the air,
Winter's dance, delicate and rare.

Frosted breath like secrets shared,
Moments treasured, feelings bared.
Crisp and clear, the world feels new,
In every flake, a dream in view.

The moon glows bright, a guardian's watch,
Embracing the cold with every touch.
As shadows waltz and twirl with grace,
We join the dance, a soft embrace.

In this stillness, hearts connect,
Warmth expands, we reflect.
The quiet dance of winter's chill,
In every breath, we find our will.

Frost-Bound Reveries

In the stillness of a chilling dawn,
Dreams weave through the frost-laden grass,
Whispers of ice-born memories,
A tapestry where time dares not pass.

Veils of silver hug the sleeping trees,
Each branch adorned in crystalline lace,
Nature's breath, a soft, breathless sigh,
As shadows undulate in silent grace.

Footprints crunch on the frozen path,
Footsteps echoing past stories untold,
The world wrapped in a shimmering shell,
A moment of beauty, quiet and bold.

Glimmers of light dance on the stream,
As day succumbs to the night's embrace,
Frost-bound dreams in a world so serene,
In this realm, we all find our place.

Beneath the stars, the silence reigns,
Each breath a tale waiting to unfold,
In the heart of winter, hope remains,
In frost-bound reveries, life is retold.

The Embrace of a Crystal Night

Under a blanket of midnight blue,
Stars twinkle like diamonds in the sky,
The moon casts shadows, soft and bright,
In the embrace of a crystal night.

Branches glimmer with frost's soft touch,
As whispers of winter kiss the air,
An enchantment stirs in the quiet dark,
Nature's beauty beyond all compare.

Footsteps guided by starlit paths,
Each step a promise of dreams to hold,
Wrapped in warmth beneath the chill,
Tales of wonder waiting to be told.

The night deepens, wrapped in the calm,
Breath visible in the still, crisp air,
Every moment a fleeting spell,
Time suspended, a world laid bare.

In the dance of the winter wind's song,
Hearts find solace, spirits take flight,
Together we wander, where we belong,
In the embrace of a crystal night.

Transcendence in Frozen Air

In the realm where silence reigns,
A world untouched by time's cruel hands,
Whispers of frost on an endless plain,
Where dreams are woven like delicate strands.

The kiss of winter upon my skin,
Breath swirls in clouds, like thoughts set free,
In every flake that dances down,
I find a piece of eternity.

Mountains rise, their peaks adorned,
With crowns of white, so proud and tall,
In this frozen expanse, reborn,
Nature's grandeur escapes our thrall.

Transcendence here, in the purest air,
As stillness settles over the day,
In the icy embrace, there's a prayer,
For moments lost, in white to stay.

With every breath, I touch the divine,
In the beauty that winter has to share,
I am one with the frost that shines,
In transcendence found in frozen air.

In the Arms of the Winter Wind

Softly the winter wind does sing,
A lullaby woven with chill and grace,
Each note a whisper, tender and bright,
Wrapped in warmth, we find our place.

Snowflakes drift like delicate dreams,
In their descent, a silent ballet,
The earth adorned in a velvety cloak,
As twilight gives way to night's display.

In the arms of the wind, we wander far,
Tracing the outlines of moonlit paths,
With laughter echoing in frozen air,
Where time stands still, and joy never halves.

Nature's embrace, a soothing balm,
To hearts that seek solace in the cold,
In the dance of the night, we find our calm,
As winter's tales are lovingly told.

So let us sway, twirl, and glide,
Bound by the magic that winter lends,
In the arms of the wind, side by side,
As our journey unravels, the soul transcends.

Frozen Horizons

In a world where silence reigns,
The frost paints pictures on the panes.
A silver glimmer, soft and bright,
As day transitions into night.

Mountains stand in icy grace,
Nature whispers in its place.
Each breath hangs in frozen air,
A tranquil moment, pure and rare.

The moon invites the stars to dance,
In the stillness, hearts advance.
Horizon meets the endless sky,
Time stands still, as moments fly.

Snowflakes waltz on chilly breeze,
A symphony among the trees.
Branches draped in white adorn,
The beauty of a winter morn.

In this land where dreams take flight,
Frozen horizons, pure delight.
In the quiet, spirits soar,
Embracing nature's endless lore.

The Serene White Horizon

A horizon wrapped in endless white,
Gentle whispers, soft twilight.
The landscape glows with purest light,
All troubles fade, all fears take flight.

Clouds drift lazily overhead,
While snowflakes fall, a soft white spread.
In the stillness, peace prevails,
As winter's beauty softly sails.

Footprints trace a path anew,
In the realm of silvery hue.
Each moment captured, tranquil, rare,
In the heart of winter's stare.

Silence blankets all around,
Nature's beauty knows no bounds.
The world awaits a springtime song,
But in this hush, we all belong.

With every breath, the magic lies,
In this serene and crisp surprise.
A horizon vast, a comforting sight,
The promise of peace in winter's light.

Wonders of the Winter Woods

Whispers echo through the trees,
Amidst the trunks, the gentle breeze.
Snowflakes dance on branches bare,
Nature's wonders, everywhere.

Footprints lead to hidden nooks,
Past frozen streams and babbling brooks.
Creatures nestled, snug and tight,
In winter's grasp, they find their light.

Icicles sparkle in the sun,
As playful shadows come undone.
The world transforms in crystal hues,
A tapestry of whites and blues.

Amidst the calm, a secret thrill,
In every drift, in every chill.
The winter woods, a sacred place,
Where time stands still and hearts embrace.

With every turn, a new surprise,
Nature's wonders, no disguise.
A peaceful heart, a peaceful mind,
In winter's woods, true joy we find.

Gentle Falling Feathers

From the sky, soft feathers fall,
Whispers of winter's gentle call.
Each one glides, a timeless art,
Filling the world, warming the heart.

A silence wraps the earth in white,
Under the glow of soft moonlight.
The landscape dressed in glimmering sheen,
A wonderland, serene and clean.

Children laugh, their spirits bright,
Chasing dreams in the fading light.
With outstretched arms, they catch the snow,
In every flake, excitement flows.

Time slows down in this sweet trance,
As winter calls us to take a chance.
To breathe it in, embrace the cold,
In gentle falling feathers, we behold.

Nature's gifts, a quiet cheer,
In every flurry, love draws near.
With every flake that meets the ground,
A magic woven all around.

Nature's Quiet Lullaby

In the whispering trees, secrets sigh,
Gentle breezes drift, oh so shy.
Crickets sing soft, under silver light,
Nature's lullaby calls through the night.

Stars twinkle down, a velvet grace,
The moon's soft glow, a warm embrace.
Rustling leaves dance in tender sway,
In nature's arms, we dream and stay.

Each petal and stone, a story told,
In the hush of night, comforts unfold.
The world slows down, breathes deep and slow,
As nature's lullaby begins to flow.

Beneath the starlit sky, peace awakes,
Echoes of life, in slumbering lakes.
Listen closely, let your heart be free,
In every whisper, feel harmony.

Nature's quiet song, a sweetest tune,
Guiding our dreams, beneath the moon.
As dawn creeps in, let it softly play,
Nature's lullaby, night turns to day.

The Stillness of Falling Snow

In a world draped white, silence falls,
Soft like a whisper, the stillness calls.
Each flake a dancer, in quiet descent,
A canvas of peace, nature's intent.

Branches bow low, with crystal coats,
A hush blankets all, the heart now floats.
Footsteps muffled on this soft embrace,
In winter's grasp, we find our place.

Time seems to pause, in this sacred space,
Where winter's breath paints with soft grace.
The world turns still, under frosted light,
Lost in the magic of pure white night.

Glistening flakes, in the moon's soft glow,
Whispers of beauty, secrets in tow.
In the chill of night, wonder can grow,
In the stillness that follows the snow.

As dawn breaks clear, the world awakes,
Each flake tells a tale, that winter makes.
In the glow of light, see shadows play,
In stillness of snow, we find our way.

Frosted Mornings

Each dawn unfurls, a frosted sheet,
Whispers of winter, in stillness greet.
Frosted glass on windows gleam,
A world transformed, like a waking dream.

Breath hangs like clouds, in crisp, cold air,
Nature wrapped tight in winter's care.
Sunlight creeps in, painting gold,
On icy branches, stories unfold.

Every step crunched, beneath furrowed feet,
Nature's symphony, in rhythm so sweet.
The world is bright, as temperatures soar,
In frosted mornings, we can't help but adore.

With every sigh, the earth comes alive,
In winter's embrace, we learn to thrive.
The beauty of ice, intricate and fine,
Frosted mornings, forever divine.

When the sun dips low, gold turns to grey,
And shadows stretch long, ending the day.
In the still of night, dreams take their flight,
Frosted mornings beckon, with soft, warm light.

Where Silence Meets the Flake

In the hush of falling, each flake lands light,
A blanket of peace, covers the night.
Whispers of winter, soft as can be,
In silence they settle, under the tree.

Gentle winds hum, a lullaby true,
Telling the secrets of what winter knew.
In shadows they dance, these crystals of white,
Where silence meets beauty, pure and bright.

A flicker of light, through the cold air shines,
Nature rejoicing in delicate designs.
Falling like dreams, in a world so still,
Where silence unfolds, with winter's chill.

As night draws near, let your heart be free,
In the calm of the snow, find serenity.
Each flake a promise, of dreams yet to make,
Where silence meets magic, in every flake.

A tapestry woven, with patience and grace,
A moment of stillness, we all can embrace.
In the lengthening shadows, warmth starts to break,
Where silence is golden, and life we remake.

Milton Keynes UK
Ingram Content Group UK Ltd.
UKHW010233111224
452348UK00011B/719